Macpherson

by Ann Lindsay Mitchell

Lang**Syne**

PUBLISHING

WRITING *to* REMEMBER

LangSyne

PUBLISHING

WRITING *to* REMEMBER

79 Main Street, Newtongrange,
Midlothian EH22 4NA
Tel: 0131 344 0414   Fax: 0845 075 6085
E-mail: info@lang-syne.co.uk
www.langsyneshop.co.uk

Design by Dorothy Meikle
Printed by Printwell Ltd
© Lang Syne Publishers Ltd 2016

ISBN 978-1-85217-078-3

Macpherson

SEPT NAMES INCLUDE:

Archibald
Clark
Clarkson
Clunie
Currie
Ellis
Ellison
Gillespie
Gillies
Gow
Gowan

Leary
MacClair
MacCleary
MacCleish
MacCurrie
MacGowan
MacKeith
MacMurdo
MacMurdoch
Pearson
Smith

Macpherson

MOTTO:
Touch not the cat but a glove.

CREST:
A Sitting Wildcat Proper.

PLANT BADGE:
White heather.

TERRITORY:
Badenoch.

Chapter one:

The origins of the clan system

by Rennie McOwan

The original Scottish clans of the Highlands and the great families of the Lowlands and Borders were gatherings of families, relatives, allies and neighbours for mutual protection against rivals or invaders.

Scotland experienced invasion from the Vikings, the Romans and English armies from the south. The Norman invasion of what is now England also had an influence on land-holding in Scotland. Some of these invaders stayed on and in time became 'Scottish'.

The word clan derives from the Gaelic language term 'clann', meaning children, and it was first used many centuries ago as communities were formed around tribal lands in glens and mountain fastnesses.

The format of clans changed over the centuries, but at its best the chief and his family held the land on behalf of all, like trustees, and the ordinary clansmen and women believed they had a blood relationship with the founder of their clan.

There were two way duties and obligations. An inadequate chief could be deposed and replaced by someone of greater ability.

Clan people had an immense pride in race. Their relationship with the chief was like adult children to a father and they had a real dignity.

The concept of clanship is very old and a more feudal notion of authority gradually crept in.

Pictland, for instance, was divided into seven principalities ruled by feudal leaders who were the strongest and most charismatic leaders of their particular groups.

By the sixth century the 'British' kingdoms of Strathclyde, Lothian and Celtic Dalriada (Argyll) had emerged and Scotland, as one nation, began to take shape in the time of King Kenneth MacAlpin.

Some chiefs claimed descent from

ancient kings which may not have been accurate in every case.

By the twelfth and thirteenth centuries the clans and families were more strongly brought under the central control of Scottish monarchs.

Lands were awarded and administered more and more under royal favour, yet the power of the area clan chiefs was still very great.

The long wars to ensure Scotland's independence against the expansionist ideas of English monarchs extended the influence of some clans and reduced the lands of others.

Those who supported Scotland's greatest king, Robert the Bruce, were awarded the territories of the families who had opposed his claim to the Scottish throne.

In the Scottish Borders country – the notorious Debatable Lands – the great families built up a ferocious reputation for providing warlike men accustomed to raiding into England and occasionally fighting one another.

Chiefs had the power to dispense justice and to confiscate lands and clan warfare produced a society where martial virtues – courage, hardiness, tenacity – were greatly admired.

Gradually the relationship between the clans and the Crown became strained as Scottish monarchs became more orientated to life in the Lowlands and, on occasion, towards England.

The Highland clans spoke a different language, Gaelic, whereas the language of Lowland Scotland and the court was Scots and in more modern times, English.

Highlanders dressed differently, had different customs, and their wild mountain land sometimes seemed almost foreign to people living in the Lowlands.

It must be emphasised that Gaelic culture was very rich and story-telling, poetry, piping, the clarsach (harp) and other music all flourished and were greatly respected.

Highland culture was different from other parts of Scotland but it was not inferior or less sophisticated.

Central Government, whether in London or Edinburgh, sometimes saw the Gaelic clans as

*"The spirit of the clan means much
to thousands of people"*

a challenge to their authority and some sent expeditions into the Highlands and west to crush the power of the Lords of the Isles.

Nevertheless, when the eighteenth century Jacobite Risings came along the cause of the Stuarts was mainly supported by Highland clans.

The word Jacobite comes from the Latin for James – Jacobus. The Jacobites wanted to restore the exiled Stuarts to the throne of Britain.

The monarchies of Scotland and England became one in 1603 when King James VI of Scotland (1st of England) gained the English throne after Queen Elizabeth died.

The Union of Parliaments of Scotland and England, the Treaty of Union, took place in 1707.

Some Highland clans, of course, and Lowland families opposed the Jacobites and supported the incoming Hanoverians.

After the Jacobite cause finally went down at Culloden in 1746 a kind of ethnic cleansing took place. The power of the chiefs was curtailed. Tartan and the pipes were banned in law.

Many emigrated, some because they

wanted to, some because they were evicted by force. In addition, many Highlanders left for the cities of the south to seek work.

Many of the clan lands became home to sheep and deer shooting estates.

But the warlike traditions of the clans and the great Lowland and Border families lived on, with their descendants fighting bravely for freedom in two world wars.

Remember the men from whence you came, says the Gaelic proverb, and to that could be added the role of many heroic women.

The spirit of the clan, of having roots, whether Highland or Lowland, means much to thousands of people.

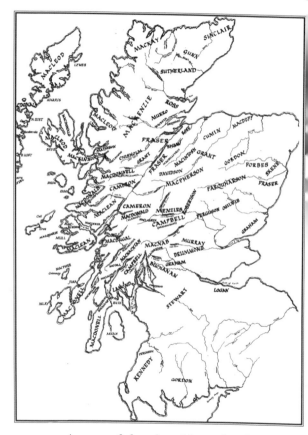

A map of the clans' homelands

Chapter two:

Sons of the parson

The Macpherson clan originated from a Mac a Phearsoin, meaning Son of the Parson. The idea that a man took his name from the son of a clergyman, in the days well before the Reformation, when the church was based solidly on Roman Catholicism is quite possible given the circumstances.

The old Celtic church was frequently responsible for clergy who could marry and, within the ancient and titled families, the role of clergyman was taken up as a matter of right by the sons and relatives of gentry. A lengthy distance from Rome no doubt helped.

So the name, Macpherson must frequently originate from widely, unrelated parts of Scotland, as many would take their name as being son of the parson in that area.

The first to appear on record, though, is one Donald Minpersuyn in 1335. He belonged to the family by the same name associated with the Argyllshire church of St Columba in Glasery. By 1420 another Macpherson was the rector in the same parish: but it is accepted that their chief of the Macpherson Clan, Macpherson of Cluny is descended from the clan Mhuirich in Strathnairn, Strathdearn and Badenoch.

These Macphersons belong to the Clan Chattan, which was a loose association of sixteen clans, descended on either male or female line from a chief called Gillechattan, whom the old Gaelic genealogists trace from Fercharthge Lond, King of Lorn, who died in 697. The Macphersons are supposed to descend from the male line, the Mackintoshes from the female line, although this is not actually proven.

The connection with the parson derives from the Gilliechattan; he is referred to as a cleric, and his progeny are mentioned as hereditary lay clergy of the areas around Kingussie. One of them, Duncan, son of Kenneth appears in 1438 as Duncan of the Parson. From him the chief of the Clan Vuireach takes the name of Macpherson.

This Duncan the parson must have been important because MacDonald, Lord of the Isles, promptly imprisoned him.

The chief of the clan was eventually recognised as the Macpherson of Cluny, first coming to notice in the 16th century, when he held huge tracts of land from Kingussie to Ben Alder and Loch Laggan, and along a stretch of the River Spey.

In 1688, a chief of Mackintosh was intent on punishing the MacDonalds for an old score. He had summoned the other chiefs to help him. The chief of the Mackintoshes would have considered himself superior to Macpherson, as in 1609 the Macpherson chiefs had signed a bond, along with all the other branches of the clan chiefs, acknowledging the Mackintosh as head of the clan Chattan.

But on this occasion Macpherson and Grant of Grant refused to assist him.

Mackintosh was furious, and before marching on to Glen Roy to do battle with the MacDonalds, he took care to make sure he wrote to the Earl of Perth, bringing this lack of subservience to his notice and requesting that the Earl of Perth should take such action as he saw fit against the two chiefs.

That night the MacDonalds assembled at Mulroy, on the tip of a hill, waiting for Mackintosh who, advancing the following morning was routed and captured. However, Macpherson of Cluny heard of this and rushed upon the MacDonalds who, too battle weary to fight, made their peace with Macpherson who insisted that Mackintosh was surrendered to him.

Mackintosh, no doubt humiliated and mortified was, however, taken by Macpherson to his home, and treated with great courtesy and charm.

This skirmish was seen in clan history as the last real clan battle.

Chapter three:

Conflicting loyalties

But if Duncan Macpherson had thought he had escaped being embroiled in any battle, he was wrong.

In 1689, he received from Lord Dundee possibly the last letter written before his death the following day at the battle of Killiecrankie.

Macpherson had been in the throes of a dilemma. His neighbours the Grants supported King William. Lord Dunfermline, the brother in law of the Duke of Gordon, Cluny's superior in Badenoch, was on the side of Claverhouse. The Mackintoshes, after initial hesitation, declared for King William. With his lands in the midst of all these opposing chieftans, Cluny knew that his land, kinsfolk and undoubtedly himself would be overwhelmed; and even used as a battleground by these differing factions.

However, while trying to avoid definite commitment, he had a month previously supported Dundee by chasing General Mackay down the Spey.

However, by hesitating long enough to avoid, almost by default, being involved at Killiecrankie, Duncan Macpherson had achieved the feat of losing no land, men, or indeed his fragile friendship with Mackintosh. Duncan died peacefully in his bed, a very old man, still with his lands intact. However, he had but one daughter, and upon his death the title passed to a cousin, whose descendant Ewan found himself in just the same type of dilemma in 1745.

Ewan decided to join the Jacobite army, and collected 300 men. His kinsman, wealthier than himself, George Macpherson of Invereshie, remained totally out of all the conflicts which followed, but Ewan, having been chivvied into action – he seemed to have taken too long to assemble his followers – by George Murray of Broughton, is next heard of at Prestonpans with 600 men, and on the retreat from Derby.

They had opposed 600 Dragoons and had many swords broken at their hilts from coming into contact with skull caps, declaring that although they wielded their swords with all their might, the skulls of the Englishmen were so thick that they could scarcely cut through them!

In the meantime, Cluny and his men kept up a much praised guerilla warfare in the areas around Badenoch to disrupt the advancing Hanoverian armies, and it was when they were so engaged that they received word about the Battle of Culloden. Cluny was in Inverness when he heard the news, his clansmen were scattered around Badenoch and they assembled and marched as speedily as possible north on the morning of 15th April, and by noon the following day were six miles from Culloden, where they were met by Cluny. Realising that they would be unable to fight after marching for a day and a half, they had a halt for rest and refreshment.

At their head was held the Bratach Uaine, a green banner. It was a well known fact that the Macphersons had yet never lost a fight when preceded by their banner, and it was widely believed that Cumberland was reputed to have been warned by a witch that if this banner reached a field of battle before himself he would lose.

As the Macphersons marched, they were met by the first of the fleeing Highlanders. Prince Charles's army was routed and the Macphersons had arrived too late to assist.

Macpherson of Cluny went into hiding. His home, Cluny Castle, was torched and destroyed. He wanted to take refuge in France, but Prince Charles implored him to stay in the Highlands and be responsible for the dispersal of the Loch Arkaig treasure. This was a sum of money, around £27,000 which the Prince had entrusted to Cluny, instructing him to disburse sums to needy fugitives, but not without first asking permission from the Prince himself.

When on board the French ship making his escape, Prince Charles wrote to Macpherson directing that £750 was to be given to various clan chiefs, and asking him to take care of various trinkets, rings, seals etc. But by September 1754, Macpherson was asked to come to Paris and bring over all the effects and whatever money was left.

Macpherson took over quite a large sum of money when he finally escaped, which, considering the destitution suffered by himself, his wife and children, was a typical example of the loyalty enjoyed by Prince Charles at the time. Cluny had hidden in a cave, about 26 feet long on the side of Creag Dhub, overlooking Lochan Ovie, then he moved to Ben Alder by Loch Ericht.

In the meantime, Ewan Macpherson continued his life on the run. His wife had given birth to their second child, a son Duncan in 1748. He was born in a corn kiln, where she was sheltering from the Hanoverian troops and ever after, Duncan was known as Duncan of the Kiln.

Ewan had several different places in which to hide. For nine years he hid in a cave built for him by his clansmen.

This cave, wrote General Stewart in his 'Sketches of the Highlanders', was in front of a woody precipice, the trees and shelving rocks completely concealing the entrance. Sir Hector Munro, obsessed with seizing his quarry stayed for two years in the Badenoch area. Ewan Macpherson, equally single minded in his efforts to stay hidden, also made sure that his wife, relatives and kinsfolk should never be implicated. He never took anyone with him when returning to a hiding place.

Ewan had close encounters with his would-be captors. His younger brother Lachlan, who by family agreement had stayed at home and not taken part in the Rising, lived at Dalchully House.

Here his wife and children were taking refuge and Ewan was in the habit of sneaking out from his cave and visiting them in the evenings. Hector Munro suspected this and one evening roused his troops and rushed to Dalchully, hoping to take Ewan by surprise.

Ewan rapidy hid any clothing which would give him away as a man of higher rank, and rushing outside in his shirt and kilt arrived just as Munro was dismounting. Ewan realised that his only chance was to brazen it out. He offered to hold the bridle of the horse, and Munro, assuming him to be a servant, left him in the courtyard, searched the house, which revealed no trace of the suspect, and when climbing up again to leave, tossed the servant a silver shilling.

This incident is commemorated in an etching on a silver platter, which was presented to the 20th Chief, another Ewan Macpherson of Cluny on his silver wedding day.

Eventually Ewan escaped to France in 1754.

Chapter four:

Restoration

Ewan's wife was a daughter of Lord Lovat, a sister of Simon Fraser and she had escaped and lived in Portugal, where he had distinguished himself as a Brigadier in the King of Portugal's army.

But as the turmoil of the '45 died down, Fraser returned to Inverness and offered to raise a regiment for the Government, which became the 71st Fraser Highlanders.

In 1761 he wrote to young 12-year-old Duncan of the Kiln offering him an ensignship in the army and Duncan wrote a letter, still preserved, in which he thanks his uncle and accepts. It does appear however, that he did not join him for a few years, as the family lived in Dunkirk until the death of Ewan in 1764.

Duncan Macpherson became a Captain in the 71st and took part in the American Wars of Independence.

Years later, he wrote of this to Colonel Stewart of Garth.

They were raised in 1775, in the short space of three months, and consisted of two battalions of 1000 rank and file each. The men were all from Scotland, and chiefly from the Highlands. There were no less than seven Chiefs in the regiment: Lovat, Lochiel, MacLeod, Mackintosh, Chisholm, Lamont and Macpherson, all of whom brought 100 men to the regiment. They got no drilling before they embarked. They had only one

fortnight's drilling at Staten Island before they were engaged with the enemy, and upon all occasions that part of the enemy opposed to them always gave way. Out of 2,200 men only 175 men came home alive.

Duncan Macpherson had already pleased the Commissioners of forfeited estates, those seized after the '45 Rebellion.

In 1784 his estates were restored to him. This was aided greatly by the efforts, loyalty and no doubt finance and influence of James Macpherson, the translator of Ossian who had in fact been offered the estates by the government, but had refused, always declaring them to be the property of Duncan.

The rejoicing in Badenoch when the estates were finally claimed back by Duncan was celebrated with bonfires and feasting.

By 1847, the 20th Chief of the Cluny Macphersons was not only able to forgive and forget the ill treatment of his forbears by both Bonnie Prince Charlie and the Hanoverian government, he was entertaining Queen Victoria and Prince

Albert at Ardverikie, an elaborate Scottish baronial house on the shores of Loch Laggan.

The Dundee Courier paid fulsome praise to Cluny in 1882, three years before his death. The occasion was a celebration for his golden wedding:-

"Cluny is the beau-ideal of a Highland chief. Winter or summer, wet or dry, finds Cluny dressed in the garb of an Old Gaul. A proficient Gaelic scholar, Cluny never speaks English when conversing with his friends in Badenoch. Of him it can be said that he speaks English as if he knew no Gaelic and Gaelic as if he were not familiar with the English tongue. Polished as any courtier in the society of the great, Cluny is equally affable and tender to, and at home among, the lowly and the poor."

His son Duncan, who succeeded him in January, 1885, as the 21st Chief, might have found such a character hard to follow, but he was to be Chief for only one year.

He was a soldier to his fingertips, serving in the Black Watch for thirty years.

As a Captain, he took part in the Indian Mutiny, and was at Cawnpore and Lucknow.

Musical relics have played a significant part in the lives of various Macphersons.

One tune for the bagpipes is entitled 'Macpherson's Lament', and is connected with a branch of the Macphersons from the area of Invereshie. The story appears to be rooted in the 17th century.

One James Macpherson was a natural son of a Macpherson of Invereshie by a beautiful gypsy girl whom he met at a wedding. James, acknowledged the child as his own, bringing him up in his own house, until he was killed chasing some cattle rustlers from his home in Badenoch.

Young James, the son, grew into a fine young man, and became a Robin Hood of the area. He lived in the Highlands, descending to raid cattle and although the acts could be deemed to be criminal, were apparently not judged to be so in the area. Harrying Lowlanders and acting with such panache were regarded as qualities of daring and bravery to be admired.

Furthermore, James was never accused of any act of cruelty, or robbing a widow, or taking from orphans. He was tall, good looking and of remarkable fitness and strength, as befits a tale of such daring. He was stronger than many of his kinsfolk, a natural leader. He wielded a sword heavier than normal, and a shield of wood, covered with bulls' hide and studded with brass nails. Legends of his fairness and prowess were whispered round the glens. It was said that he gave the spoils from the rich to aid the poor, and acts of potential violence between his kinsfolk were deflected by the sheer strength of James Macpherson's arms.

But it was a dispute with a particularly lawless kinsman, who betrayed him, which brought about his downfall.

A Warrant for his arrest was issued, but James escaped, much to the annoyance of the magistrates in Aberdeen. They bribed a pretty girl in Aberdeen to lure him into a trap, but with the assistance of gypsy Peter Brown, and his cousin Donald Macpherson, he escaped.

But it was a matter of time before he was caught, this time in a rioting expedition to Keith market, along with Peter Brown and two cousins.

Grant of Grant, who was a friend of the Macphersons tried to save him from the gallows, and a reprieve was on its way, but the Sheriff of Banff, knowing of its arrival, managed to both delay the messenger and hasten on the execution. (As a result the town of Banff was deprived of its power to try and execute offenders for many years.)

Just before Macpherson knew he was about to hang, he composed the tune 'Macpherson's Lament' and asked if there was anyone in the crowd gathered to see his execution who would take possession and care for his much loved fiddle, at which he was also legendary as a fine player.

Frightened of the consequences, no-one came forward whereupon Macpherson smashed the fiddle to pieces. The shaft was rescued and preserved for years in Cluny Castle and joined the other relics of the Macpherson clan.